Samuel French Acting Edition

G000154832

The Happy Journey to
Trenton and Camden

by Thornton Wilder

SAMUELFRENCH.COM   SAMUELFRENCH.CO.UK

FOR PRODUCTION ENQUIRIES

UNITED STATES AND CANADA
Info@SamuelFrench.com
1-866-598-8449

UNITED KINGDOM AND EUROPE
Plays@SamuelFrench.co.uk
020-7255-4302

Each title is subject to availability from Samuel French, depending upon country of performance. Please be aware that *THE HAPPY JOURNEY TO TRENTON AND CAMDEN* may not be licensed by Samuel French in your territory. Professional and amateur producers should contact the nearest Samuel French office or licensing partner to verify availability.

MUSIC USE NOTE

IMPORTANT BILLING AND CREDIT REQUIREMENTS

Introduction to Thornton Wilder's
Happy Journey to Trenton and Camden

Happy Journey to Trenton and Camden is one of six one-act plays that the thirty four-year-old Thornton Wilder published in 1931—in the United States and in England—under the title *The Long Christmas Dinner and Other Plays in One Act*. Each play celebrates different theatrical forms and moods. Today, acknowledging their distinguished place in both the history of twentieth-century drama and in Wilder's six decades as a practicing artist, we call them *Wilder's Classic One Acts*: *The Long Christmas Dinner, Queens of France, Pullman Car Hiawatha, Love and How to Cure It, Such Things Only Happen in Books,* and *The Happy Journey to Trenton and Camden.*

***

Wilder always wanted to write plays and wasted little time getting started. By the time he graduated from college in 1920 he had already published some twenty pieces of short drama and one major play— to say nothing of being prodigiously well read in theater, haunting many a stage, and even serving a stint as a paid theatre critic for a noted Boston newspaper. But when these six plays were published, few beyond an inner-circle thought of Wilder as a playwright. (*Our Town,* his first full-length drama to reach Broadway, lay seven years in the future, opening February 4, 1938). Everyone, however, knew Thornton Wilder as a novelist, the writer who had given the world three novels, including the acclaimed 1927 Pulitzer Prize-winning *The Bridge of San Luis Rey.*

Wilder's lack of public status as a dramatist notwithstanding, fans of his fiction and others eagerly purchased his newest offering. Sales of *The Long Christmas Dinner and Other Plays in One Act* were strong, as was critical response. (For example, the influential *New York Times* reviewer Percy

Hutchison declared the plays "very near to miniatures masterpieces".) Plays, of course, show best when performed, and after Samuel French added the titles to its catalogue in 1932, productions of these works began springing up across the country and in England.

Each of *Wilder's Classic One Acts* is a polished and masterful example of drama in the compressed form. In these mini-masterpieces, we find Wilder experimenting with such innovative ideas as the stage-manager as a visible and engaged character, non-linear time schemes, the banishment of literal scenery, and elements drawn from Classical theatre, farce and comedy. Wilder would later employ these techniques in his four major plays: *Our Town* (1938), *The Merchant of Yonkers/The Matchmaker* (1938/1954), *The Skin of our Teeth* (1942) and *The Alcestiad* (1955), his unfinished adaptation of George Farquhar's *The Beaux' Stratagem* (1939) and his fourth novel, *Heaven's My Destination* (1935). When performing Wilder's one acts, actors therefore find themselves not only handling theatrical tools that contributed to a lasting chapter in the history of twentieth century drama and fiction, but also exploring ancient and honorable theatrical styles.

Although they were written for schools and community playhouses, the official record of these plays, with the exception of *Such Things Only Happen in Books*[*], includes professional productions, adaptations for radio, television, and in the case of *The Long Christmas Dinner*, even opera. Perhaps the most high-profile production of any of the six was the successful Broadway run of *The Happy Journey to Trenton and Camden*, as the lively curtain-raiser for Jean-Paul Sartre's notorious *The Respectful Prostitute* in 1947. Given

---

[*] When it was first produced, Wilder described *Such Things Only Happen in Books*, a play he purposely (and playfully) constructed in a conventional form, as "an attempt to see how many plots may be worked into one act." By the late 1930s, for reasons never explained, he had withdrawn it. It remained in this status until 1997 when Wilder's literary executor restored it to the Wilder canon.

their stature, it is no surprise that over the past half-century, several of the six have turned up regularly off-Broadway, where they have won critical acclaim and awards.

***

Samuel French and the Wilder family take great pleasure and pride in celebrating *Wilder's Classics One-Acts*, now in their eighth decade, by reissuing them in new collected and individual acting editions. For additional information about these works please visit www.thorntonwilder.com.

Tappan Wilder
Literary Executor for Thornton Wilder

CHARACTERS

THE STAGE MANAGER

MA, Mrs. Kate Kirby

ARTHUR, thirteen, her son

CAROLINE, fifteen, her daughter

PA

BEULAH, twenty-two, the Kirbys' married daughter who lives in Camden, New Jersey

SETTING

The Kirby house; then the Kirby family car trip from Newark to Camden, New Jersey.

NOTES TO THE PRODUCER

Although the speech, manner and business of the actors is colloquial and realistic, the production should stimulate the imagination and be implied and suggestive. All properties, except two, are imaginary, but their use is to be carried with detailed pantomime. One of these two is the automobile, which is made up of four chairs on a low platform. In some productions, because of the sight lines of the auditorium, it has been found necessary to raise slightly the two rear chairs of the automobile. The second is an ordinary cot or couch.

The Stage Manager not only moves forward and withdraws these two properties, but he reads from a typescript the lines of all the minor (invisible) characters. He reads them clearly, but with little attempt at characterization, even when he responds in the person of a child or a woman. He may smoke, read a newspaper and eat an apple throughout the course of the play. He should never be obtrusive nor distract the attention of the audience from the central action.

It should constantly be borne in mind that the purpose of this play is the portrayal of the character of Ma Kirby, the author at one time having even considered entitling the play "The Portrait of a Lady." Accordingly, the director should constantly keep in mind that Ma Kirby's humor, strength and humanity constitute the unifying element throughout. This aspect should always rise above the merely humorous characteristic details of the play.

Many productions have fallen into two regrettable extremes. On the one hand actors have exaggerated the humorous characters and situations in the direction of farce; and on the other hand, have treated Ma Kirby's sentiment and religion with sentimentality and preachy solemnity. The atmosphere, comedy, and characterization of this play are most effective when they are handled with great simplicity and evenness.

Thornton Wilder, 1931

(No scenery is required for this play. The idea is that no place is being represented. This may be achieved by a gray curtain back-drop with no side-pieces; a cyclorama; or the empty bare stage.)

(As the curtain rises **THE STAGE MANAGER** *is leaning lazily against the proscenium pillar at the audiences left. He is smoking.)*

*(***ARTHUR*** *is playing marbles in the center of the stage in pantomime.)*

*(***CAROLINE*** *is at the remote back right talking to some girls who are invisible to us.)*

*(***MA KIRBY*** *is anxiously putting on her hat [real] before an imaginary mirror.)*

MA. Where's your pa? Why isn't he here? I declare we'll never get started.

ARTHUR. Ma, where's my hat? I guess I don't go if I can't find my hat. *(still playing marbles)*

MA. Go out into the hall and see if it isn't there. Where's Caroline gone to now, the plagued child?

ARTHUR. She's out waitin' in the street talkin' to the Jones girls. – I just looked in the hall a thousand times, Ma, and it isn't there. *(He spits for good luck before a difficult shot and mutters:)* Come on, baby.

MA. Go and look again, I say. Look carefully.

*(***ARTHUR*** *rises, runs to the right, turns around swiftly, returns to his game, flinging himself on the floor with a terrible impact and starts shooting an aggie.)*

ARTHUR. No, Ma, it's not there.

MA. *(serenely)* Well, you don't leave Newark without that hat, make up your mind to that. I don't go no journeys with a hoodlum.

9

ARTHUR. Aw, Ma!

(**MA** *comes down to the footlights and talks toward the audience as through a window.*)

MA. *(calling)* Oh, Mrs. Schwartz!

THE STAGE MANAGER. *(consulting his script)* Here I am, Mrs. Kirby. Are you going yet?

MA. I guess we're going in just a minute. How's the baby?

THE STAGE MANAGER. She's all right now. We slapped her on the back and she spat it up.

MA. Isn't that fine! – Well now, if you'll be good enough to give the cat a saucer of milk in the morning and the evening, Mrs. Schwartz, I'll be ever so grateful to you. – Oh, good afternoon, Mrs. Hobmeyer!

THE STAGE MANAGER. Good afternoon, Mrs. Kirby, I hear you're going away.

MA. *(modest)* Oh, just for three days, Mrs. Hobmeyer, to see my married daughter, Beulah, in Camden. Elmer's got his vacation week from the laundry early this year, and he's just the best driver in the world.

(**CAROLINE** *comes "into the house" and stands by her mother.*)

THE STAGE MANAGER. Is the whole family going?

MA. Yes, all four of us that's here. The change ought to be good for the children. My married daughter was downright sick a while ago –

THE STAGE MANAGER. Tchk-Tchk-Tchk! Yes. I remember you tellin' us.

MA. And I just want to go down and see the child. I ain't seen her since then. I just won't rest easy in my mind without I see her. *(to* **CAROLINE***)* Can't you say good afternoon to Mrs. Hobmeyer?

CAROLINE. *(blushes and lowers her eyes and says woodenly)* Good afternoon, Mrs. Hobmeyer.

THE STAGE MANAGER. Good afternoon, dear. – Well, I'll wait and beat these rugs after you're gone, because I don't want to choke you. I hope you have a good time and find everything all right.

MA. Thank you, Mrs. Hobmeyer, I hope I will. – Well, I guess that milk for the cat is all, Mrs. Schwartz, if you're sure you don't mind. If anything should come up, the key to the back door is hanging by the icebox.

CAROLINE. Ma! Not so loud.

ARTHUR. Everybody can hear yuh.

MA. Stop pullin' my dress, children. *(in a loud whisper)* The key to the back door I'll leave hangin' by the icebox and I'll leave the screen door unhooked.

THE STAGE MANAGER. Now have a good trip, dear, and give my love to Loolie.

MA. I will, and thank you a thousand times.

*(She lowers the window, turns up stage and looks around. **CAROLINE** goes left and vigorously rubs her cheeks. **MA** occupies herself with the last touches of packing.)*

What can be keeping your pa?

ARTHUR. *(who has not left his marbles)* I can't find my hat, Ma.

*(Enter **ELMER** holding a hat.)*

ELMER. Here's Arthur's hat. He musta left it in the car Sunday.

MA. That's a mercy. Now we can start. – Caroline Kirby, what you done to your cheeks?

CAROLINE. *(defiant, abashed)* Nothin'.

MA. If you've put anything on 'em, I'll slap you.

CAROLINE. No, Ma, of course I haven't. *(hanging her head)* I just rubbed 'em to make 'em red. All the girls do that at high school when they're goin' places.

MA. Such silliness I never saw. Elmer, what kep' you?

ELMER. *(always even-voiced and always looking out a little anxiously through his spectacles)* I just went to the garage and had Charlie give a last look at it, Kate.

MA. I'm glad you did. *(collecting two pieces of imaginary luggage and starting for the door)* I wouldn't like to have no breakdown miles from anywhere. Now we can start. Arthur, put those marbles away. Anybody'd think you didn't want to go on a journey to look at yuh.

(They go out through the "hall," take the short steps that denote going downstairs, and find themselves in the street.)

ELMER. Here, you boys, you keep away from that car.

MA. Those Sullivan boys put their heads into everything.

(THE STAGE MANAGER has moved forward four chairs and a low platform. This is the automobile. It is in the center of the stage and faces the audience. The platform slightly raises the two chairs in the rear. PA's hands hold an imaginary steering wheel and continually shift gears. CAROLINE sits beside him. ARTHUR is behind him and MA behind CAROLINE)

CAROLINE. *(self-consciously)* Good-bye, Mildred. Good-bye, Helen.

THE STAGE MANAGER. Good-bye, Caroline. Good-bye, Mrs. Kirby. I hope y'have a good time.

MA. Good-bye, girls.

THE STAGE MANAGER. Good-bye, Kate. The car looks fine.

MA. *(looking upward toward a window)* Oh, good-bye, Emma! *(modestly)* We think it's the best little Chevrolet in the world. – Oh, good-bye, Mrs. Adler!

THE STAGE MANAGER. What, are you going away, Mrs. Kirby?

MA. Just for three days, Mrs. Adler, to see my married daughter in Camden.

THE STAGE MANAGER. Have a good time.

(Now MA, CAROLINE and THE STAGE MANAGER break out into a tremendous chorus of good-byes. The whole street is saying good-bye. ARTHUR takes out his peashooter and lets fly happily into the air. There is a lurch or two and they are off.)

ARTHUR. *(in sudden fright)* Pa! Pa! Don't go by the school. Mr. Biedenbach might see us!

MA. I don't care if he does see us. I guess I can take my children out of school for one day without having to hide down back streets about it.

*(***ELMER*** *nods to a passerby.* **MA** *asks without sharpness.)*

Who was that you spoke to, Elmer?

ELMER. That was the fellow who arranges our banquets down to the lodge, Kate.

MA. Is he the one who had to buy four hundred steaks? *(***PA*** *nods.)* I declare, I'm glad I'm not him.

ELMER. The air's getting better already. Take deep breaths, children.

(They inhale noisily.)

ARTHUR. *(pointing to a sign and indicating that it gradually goes by)* Gee, it's almost open fields already. "*Weber and Heilbronner Suits for Well-Dressed Men.*" Ma, can I have one of them some day?

MA. If you graduate with good marks perhaps your father'll let you have one for graduation.

(Pause. General gazing about and then a sudden lurch.)

CAROLINE. *(whining)* Oh, Pa! Do we have to wait while that whole funeral goes by?

*(***PA*** *takes off his hat.* **MA** *cranes forward with absorbed curiosity.)*

MA. Take off your hat, Arthur. Look at your father. – Why, Elmer, I do believe that's a lodge brother of yours. See the banner? I suppose this is the Elizabeth branch.

*(***ELMER*** *nods.* **MA** *sighs Tchk-tchk-tchk. They all lean forward and watch the funeral in silence, growing momentarily more solemnized. After a pause,* **MA** *continues almost dreamily but not sentimentaly:)*

Well, we haven't forgotten the funeral that we went on, have we? We haven't forgotten our good Harold. He gave his life for his country, we mustn't forget that.

(She passes her finger from the corner of her eye across her cheek. There is another pause, with cheerful resignation.)

MA. *(cont.)* Well, we'll all hold up the traffic for a few minutes some day.

THE CHILDREN. *(very uncomfortable)* Ma!

MA. *(without self-pity)* Well I'm "ready," children. I hope everybody in this car is "ready."

*(She puts her hand on **PA**'s shoulder.)*

And I pray to go first, Elmer. Yes.

*(**PA** touches her hand.)*

CAROLINE. Ma, everybody's looking at you.

ARTHUR. Everybody's laughing at you.

MA. Oh, hold your tongues! I don't care what a lot of silly people in Elizabeth, New Jersey, think of me. – Now we can go on. That's the last.

(There is another lurch and the car goes on.)

CAROLINE. *(looking at a sign and turning as she passes it)* "Fit-Rite Suspenders. The Working Man's Choice." Pa, why do they spell Rite that way?

ELMER. So that it'll make you stop and ask about it, Missy.

CAROLINE. Papa, you're teasing me. – Ma, why do they say "Three Hundred Rooms Three Hundred Baths?"

ARTHUR. "Millers Spaghetti: The Family's Favorite Dish." Ma, why don't you ever have spaghetti?

MA. Go along, you'd never eat it.

ARTHUR. Ma, I like it now.

CAROLINE. *(with gesture)* Yum-yum. It looks wonderful up there. Ma, make some when we get home?

MA. *(dryly)* "The management is always happy to receive suggestions. We aim to please."

*(The whole family finds this exquisitely funny. The children scream with laughter. Even **ELMER** smiles. **MA** remains modest)*

ELMER. Well, I guess no one's complaining, Kate. Everybody knows you're a good cook.

MA. I don't know whether I'm a good cook or not, but I know I've had practice. At least I've cooked three meals a day for twenty-five years.

ARTHUR. Aw, Ma, you went out to eat once in a while.

MA. Yes. That made it a leap year.

(This joke is no less successful than its predecessor. When the laughter dies down, **CAROLINE** *turns around in an ecstasy of well-being, and kneeling on the cushions says.)*

CAROLINE. Ma, I love going out in the country like this. Let's do it often, Ma.

MA. Goodness, smell that air will you! It's got the whole ocean in it. – Elmer, drive careful over that bridge. This must be New Brunswick we're coming to.

ARTHUR. *(jealous of his mother's successes)* Ma, when is the next comfort station?

MA. *(unruffled)* You don't want one. You just said that to be awful.

CAROLINE. *(shrilly)* Yes, he did, Ma. He's terrible. He says that kind of thing right out in school and I want to sink through the floor, Ma. He's terrible.

MA. Oh, don't get so excited about nothing, Miss Proper! I guess we're all yewman-beings in this car, at least as far as I know. And, Arthur, you try and be a gentleman. – Elmer, don't run over that collie dog.

(She follows the dog with her eyes.)

Looked kinda peaked to me. Needs a good honest bowl of leavings. Pretty dog, too.

(Her eyes fall on a billboard.)

That's a pretty advertisement for Chesterfield cigarettes, isn't it? Looks like Beulah, a little.

ARTHUR. Ma?

MA. Yes.

ARTHUR. Can't I take a paper route *("route" rhymes with "out")* with the *Newark Daily Post?*

MA. No, you cannot. No, sir. I hear they make the paperboys get up at four-thirty in the morning. No son of mine is going to get up at four-thirty every morning, not if it's to make a million dollars. Your *Saturday Evening Post* route on Thursday mornings is enough.

ARTHUR. Aw, Ma.

MA. No, sir. No son of mine is going to get up at four-thirty and miss the sleep God meant him to have.

ARTHUR. *(sullenly)* Hhm! Ma's always talking about God. I guess she got a letter from him this morning.

(MA rises, outraged.)

MA. Elmer, stop that automobile this minute. I don't go another step with anybody that says things like that. Arthur, you get out of this car. *(PA stops the car.)* Elmer, you give him a dollar bill. He can go back to Newark, by himself. I don't want him.

ARTHUR. What did I say? There wasn't anything terrible about that.

ELMER. I didn't hear what he said, Kate.

MA. God has done a lot of things for me and I won't have Him made fun of by anybody. Get out of the car this minute.

CAROLINE. Aw, Ma – don't spoil the ride.

MA. No.

ELMER. We might as well go on, Kate, since we've got started. I'll talk to the boy tonight.

MA. *(slowly conceding)* All right, if you say so, Elmer. *(PA starts the car.)* But I won't sit beside him. Caroline, you come, and sit by me.

ARTHUR. *(frightened)* Aw, Ma, that wasn't so terrible.

MA. I don't want to talk about it. I hope your father washes your mouth out with soap and water. – Where'd we all be if I started talking about God like that, I'd like to know! We'd be in the speakeasies and nightclubs and places like that, that's where we'd be. – All right, Elmer, you can go on now.

CAROLINE. *(after a slight pause)* What did he say, Ma? I didn't hear what he said.

MA. I don't want to talk about it.

(They drive on in silence for a moment, the shocked silence after a scandal.)

ELMER. I'm going to stop and give the car a little water, I guess.

MA. All right, Elmer. You know best.

ELMER. *(turns the wheel and stops; to a garage hand:)* Could I have a little water in the radiator – to make sure?

THE STAGE MANAGER. *(In this scene alone he lays aside his script and enters into a role seriously.)* You sure can. *(He punches the tires.)* Air, all right? Do you need any oil or gas?

ELMER. No, I think not. I just got fixed up in Newark.

MA. We're on the right road for Camden, are we?

THE STAGE MANAGER. Yes, keep straight ahead. You can't miss it. You'll be in Trenton in a few minutes.

(He carefully pours some water into the hood.)

Camden's a great town, lady, believe me.

MA. My daughter likes it fine – my married daughter.

THE STAGE MANAGER. Yea? It's a great burg all right. I guess I think so because I was born near there.

MA. Well, well. Your folks still live there?

THE STAGE MANAGER. *(Standing with one foot on the rung of* **MA***'s chair. They have taken a great fancy to one another.)* No, my old man sold the farm and they built a factory on it. So the folks moved to Philadelphia.

MA. My married daughter Beulah lives there because her husband works in the telephone company. – Stop pokin' me, Caroline! – We're all going down to see her for a few days.

THE STAGE MANAGER. Yea?

MA. She's been sick, you see, and I just felt I had to go and see her. My husband and my boy are going to stay at the Y.M.C.A. I hear they've got a dormitory on the top floor that's real clean and comfortable. Had you ever been there?

THE STAGE MANAGER. No. I'm Knights of Columbus myself.

MA. Oh.

THE STAGE MANAGER. I used to play basketball at the Y though. It looked all right to me.

(He reluctantly shakes himself out of it and pretends to examine the car again, whistling.)

Well, I guess you're all set now, lady. I hope you have a good trip; you can't miss it.

EVERYBODY. Thanks. Thanks a lot. Good luck to you.

(The car jolts and lurches.)

MA. *(with a sigh)* The world's full of nice people. – That's what I call a nice young man.

CAROLINE. *(earnestly)* Ma, you oughtn't to tell 'em all everything about yourself.

MA. Well, Caroline, you do your way and I'll do mine. – He looked kinda pale to me. I'd like to feed him up for a few days. His mother lives in Philadelphia and I expect he eats at those dreadful Greek places.

CAROLINE. I'm hungry. Pa, there's a hot dog stand. K'n I have one?

ELMER. We'll all have one, eh, Kate? We had such an early lunch.

MA. Just as you think best, Elmer.

(He stops the car.)

ELMER. Arthur, here's half a dollar. Run over and see what they have. Not too much mustard either.

*(**ARTHUR** descends from the car and goes offstage right. **MA** and **CAROLINE** get out and walk a bit.)*

MA. What's that flower over there? I'll take some of those to Beulah.

CAROLINE. It's just a weed, Ma.

MA. I like it. – My, look at the sky, wouldya! I'm glad I was born in New Jersey. I've always said it was the best state in the Union. Every state has something no other state has got.

(They stroll about humming. Presently **ARTHUR** *returns with his hands full of imaginary hot dogs which he distributes. He is still very much cast down by the recent scandal. He finally approaches his mother and says falteringly:)*

ARTHUR. Ma, I'm sorry. I'm sorry for what I said.

(He bursts into tears and puts his forehead against her elbow.)

MA. There. There. We all say wicked things at times. I know you didn't mean it like it sounded.

(He weeps still more violently than before.)

Why, now, now! I forgive you, Arthur, and tonight before you go to bed you... *(She whispers.)* You're a good boy at heart, Arthur, and we all know it.

*(***CAROLINE** *starts to cry too.* **MA** *is suddenly joyously alive and happy.)*

Sakes alive, it's too nice a day for us all to be cryin'. Come now, get in. Caroline, go up in front with your father. Ma wants to sit with her beau.

*(***CAROLINE** *sits in front with her father.* **MA** *lets* **ARTHUR** *get in car ahead of her; then she closes door.)*

I never saw such children. Your hot dogs are all getting wet. Now chew them fine, everybody. – All right, Elmer, forward march.

(Car starts. **CAROLINE** *spits.)*

– Caroline, whatever are you doing?

CAROLINE. I'm spitting out the leather, Ma.

MA. Then say Excuse me.

CAROLINE. Excuse me, please. *(She spits again.)*

MA. What's this place? Arthur, did you see the post office?

ARTHUR. It said Lawrenceville.

MA. Hnn. School kinda. Nice. I wonder what that big yellow house set back was. – Now it's beginning to be Trenton.

CAROLINE. Papa, it was near here that George Washington crossed the Delaware. It was near Trenton, Mama. He was first in war and first in peace and first in the hearts of his countrymen.

MA. *(surveying the passing world, serene and didactic)* Well, the thing I like about him best was that he never told a lie.

(The children are duly cast down. There is a pause.)

There's a sunset for you. There's nothing like a good sunset.

ARTHUR. There's an Ohio license in front of us. Ma, have you ever been to Ohio?

MA. No.

(A dreamy silence descends upon them. CAROLINE sits closer to her father. MA puts her arm around ARTHUR, unsentimentally.)

ARTHUR. Ma, what a lotta people there are in the world, Ma. There must be thousands and thousands in the United States. Ma, how many are there?

MA. I don't know. Ask your father.

ARTHUR. Pa, how many are there?

ELMER. There are a hundred and twenty-six million, Kate.

MA. *(giving a pressure about ARTHUR's shoulder)* And they all like to drive out in the evening with their children beside 'em.

(another pause)

Why doesn't somebody sing something? Arthur, you're always singing something; what's the matter with you?

ARTHUR. All right. What'll we sing? *(He sketches:)*

In the Blue Ridge mountains of Virginia,
On the trail of the lonesome pine...
No, I don't like that anymore. Let's do:
I been workin' on de railroad

(CAROLINE *joins in.*)

All de liblong day.

(MA *sings.*)

, I been workin' on de railroad

(PA *joins in.*)

Just to pass de time away.

(MA *suddenly jumps up with a wild cry.*)

MA. Elmer, that signpost said Camden, I saw it.

ELMER. All right, Kate, if you're sure.

(*much shifting of gears, backing, and jolting*)

MA. Yes, there it is. Camden – five miles. Dear old Beulah.
(The journey continues.) – Now, children, you be good
and quiet during dinner. She's just got out of bed after
a big sorta operation, and we must all move around
kinda quiet. First you drop me and Caroline at the
door and just say hello, and then you menfolk go over
to the Y.M.C.A. and come back for dinner in about an
hour.

CAROLINE. *(shutting her eyes and pressing her fists passionately
against her nose)* I see the first star. Everybody make a
wish.

Star light, star bright,

First star I seen tonight.

I wish I may, I wish I might

Have the wish I wish tonight.

(then solemnly) Pins. Mama, you say "needles."

(*She interlocks little fingers with her mother.*)

MA. Needles.

CAROLINE. Shakespeare. Ma, you say "Longfellow."

MA. Longfellow.

CAROLINE. Now it's a secret and I can't tell it to anybody. Ma, you make a wish.

MA. *(with almost grim humor)* No, I can make wishes without waiting for no star. And I can tell my wishes right out loud too. Do you want to hear them?

CAROLINE. *(resignedly)* No, Ma, we know 'em already. We've heard 'em.

(She hangs her head affectedly on her mother's left shoulder and says with unmalicious mimicry.)

You want me to be a good girl and you want Arthur to be honest in word and deed.

MA. *(majestically)* Yes. So mind yourself.

ELMER. Caroline, take out that letter from Beulah in my coat pocket by you and read aloud the places I marked with red pencil.

CAROLINE. *(working)* "A few blocks after you pass the two big oil tanks on your left…"

EVERYBODY. *(pointing backward)* There they are!

CAROLINE. "…you come to a corner where there's an A & P store on the left and a firehouse kitty-corner to it…"

(They all jubilantly identify these landmarks.)

"…turn right, go two blocks, and our house is Weyerhauser Street Number 471."

MA. It's an even nicer street than they used to live in. And right handy to an A & P.

CAROLINE. *(whispering)* Ma, it's better than our street. It's richer than our street. – Ma, isn't Beulah richer than we are?

MA. *(looking at her with a firm and glassy eye)* Mind yourself, missy. I don't want to hear anybody talking about rich or not rich when I'm around. If people aren't nice I don't care how rich they are. I live in the best street in the world because my husband and children live there.

*(She glares impressively at **CAROLINE** a moment to let this lesson sink in, then looks up, sees **BEULAH** and waves.)*

There's Beulah standing on the steps lookin' for us.

(**BEULAH** *has appeared and is waving. They all call out "Hello, Beulah – Hello." Presently they are all getting out of the car.*)

BEULAH. Hello, Mama. – Well, lookit how Arthur and Caroline are growing!

MA. They're bursting all their clothes!

BEULAH. *(kisses her father long and affectionately)* Hello, Papa. Good old Papa. You look tired, Pa –

MA. – Yes, your pa needs a rest. Thank Heaven, his vacation has come just now. We'll feed him up and let him sleep late. Pa has a present for you, Loolie. He would go and buy it.

BEULAH. Why, Pa, you're terrible to go and buy anything for me. Isn't he terrible?

MA. Well, it's a secret. You can open it at dinner.

BEULAH. *(puts her arm around his neck and rubs her nose against his temple)* Crazy old Pa, goin' buyin' things! It's me that ought to be buyin' things for you, Pa.

ELMER. Oh, no! There's only one Loolie in the world.

BEULAH. *(whispering, as her eyes fill with tears)* Are you glad I'm still alive, Pa?

(She kisses him abruptly and goes back to the house steps.)

ELMER. Where's Horace, Loolie?

BEULAH. He was kep' over a little at the office. He'll be here any minute. He's crazy to see you all.

MA. All right. You men go over to the Y and come back in about an hour.

BEULAH. *(As her father returns to the wheel, she stands out in the street beside him.)* Go straight along, Pa, you can't miss it. It just stares at ya.

*(***THE STAGE MANAGER*** removes the automobile with the help of **PA** and **ARTHUR**, who go off waving their good-byes.)*

Well, come on upstairs, Ma, and take off your things. Caroline, there's a surprise for you in the backyard.

CAROLINE. Rabbits?

BEULAH. No.

CAROLINE. Chickens?

BEULAH. No. Go and see.

(CAROLINE runs offstage. BEULAH and MA gradually go upstairs.)

There are two new puppies. You be thinking over whether you can keep one in Newark.

MA. I guess we can.

(THE STAGE MANAGER pushes out a bed from the left. Its foot is toward the right.)

It's a nice house, Beulah. You just got a lovely home.

BEULAH. When I got back from the hospital, Horace had moved everything into it, and there wasn't anything for me to do.

MA. It's lovely.

(BEULAH sits on bed, testing the springs.)

BEULAH. I think you'll find this comfortable, Ma.

MA. *(taking off her hat)* Oh, I could sleep on a heapa shoes, Loolie! I don't have no trouble sleepin'.

(She sits down beside her.)

Now let me look at my girl. Well, well, when I last saw you, you didn't know me. You kep' saying: "When's Mama comin'? When's Mama comin'?" But the doctor sent me away.

BEULAH. *(puts her head on her mother's shoulder and weeps)* It was awful, Mama. It was awful. She didn't even live a few minutes, Mama. It was awful.

MA. *(looking far away)* God thought best, dear. God thought best. We don't understand why. We just go on, honey, doin' our business.

(then almost abruptly-passing the back of her hand across her cheek) Well, now, what are we giving the men to eat tonight?

BEULAH. There's a chicken in the oven.

MA. What time didya put it in?

BEULAH. *(restraining her)* Aw, Ma, don't go yet. *(taking her mother's hand and drawing her down beside her)* I like to sit here with you this way. You always get the fidgets when we try and pet ya, Mama.

MA. *(ruefully, laughing)* Yes, it's kinda foolish. I'm just an old Newark bag-a-bones.

(She glances at the backs of her hands.)

BEULAH. *(indignantly)* Why, Ma, you're good-lookin'! We always said you were good-lookin'. – And besides, you're the best ma we could ever have.

MA. *(uncomfortable)* Well, I hope you like me. There's nothin' like being liked by your family. *(rises)* – Now I'm going downstairs to look at the chicken. You stretch out here for a minute and shut your eyes. – Have you got everything laid in for breakfast before the shops close?

BEULAH. Oh, you know! Ham and eggs.

*(They both laugh. **MA** puts an imaginary blanket over **BEULAH**.)*

MA. I declare I never could understand what men see in ham and eggs. I think they're horrible. – What time did you put the chicken in?

BEULAH. Five o'clock.

MA. Well, now, you shut your eyes for ten minutes.

*(**BEULAH** stretches out and shuts her eyes. **MA** descends the stairs absentmindedly singing.)*

"There were ninety and nine that safely lay
In the shelter of the fold,
But one was out on the hills away,
Far off from the gates of gold…"

End of Play

THORNTON WILDER

Thornton Wilder (1897–1975) was a pivotal figure in the literary history of the twentieth-century. He is the only writer to win Pulitzer Prizes for both fiction and drama. He received the Pulitzer for his novel *The Bridge of San Luis Rey* (1927) and the plays *Our Town* (1938) and *The Skin of Our Teeth* (1942). His other best-selling novels include *The Cabala, The Woman of Andros, Heaven's My Destination, The Ides of March, The Eighth Day* and *Theophilus North.* His other major dramas include *The Matchmaker* (adapted as the musical *Hello, Dolly!*) and *The Alcestiad. The Happy Journey to Trenton and Camden, Pullman Car Hiawatha* and *The Long Christmas Dinner* are among his well-known shorter plays.

Wilder's many honors include the Gold Medal for Fiction from the American Academy of Arts and Letters, the Presidential Medal of Freedom, the National Book Committee's Medal for Literature and the Goethe-Plakette Award (Germany).

Wilder was born in Madison, Wisconsin, on April 17, 1897. He spent part of his boyhood in China and was educated principally in California, graduating from Berkeley High School in 1915. After attending Oberlin College for two years, he transferred to Yale, where he received his BA in 1920. His post-graduate studies included a year spent studying archaeology and Italian at the American Academy in Rome (1920-21) and graduate work in French at Princeton (Master's degree, 1926).

In addition to his talents as a playwright and novelist, Wilder was an accomplished essayist, translator, research scholar, teacher, lecturer, librettist and screenwriter. In 1942, he teamed with Alfred Hitchcock on the classic psycho-thriller *Shadow of a Doubt.* Versed in foreign languages, he translated and adapted plays by Ibsen, Sartre and Obey. He read and spoke German, French and Spanish, and his scholarship included significant research on James Joyce and Lope de Vega. Wilder enjoyed acting and played major roles in several of his plays in summer theater productions. He also possessed a lifelong love of music and wrote librettos for two operas based on *The Long Christmas Dinner* (composer Paul Hindemith) and *The Alcestiad* (composer Louis Talma). One of Wilder's deepest passions was teaching. He began this career in 1921 as an instructor in French at The Lawrenceville School in New Jersey.

During the 1930s he taught courses in Classics in Translation and Composition at the University of Chicago. In 1950–51, he served as the Charles Eliot Norton Professor of Poetry at Harvard. During WWII, Wilder served in Army Air Force Intelligence. He was awarded the Legion of Merit Bronze Star, the Legion d'honneur and the Order of the British Empire.

In 1930, with royalties received from *The Bridge of San Luis Rey*, Wilder built a home for himself and his family in Hamden, Connecticut. Although often away from home, up to as many as 250 days a year, restlessly seeking quiet places in which to write, he always returned to "The House that the Bridge Built." He died here on December 7, 1975.

Also by
Thornton Wilder

The Alcestiad
The Beaux' Stratagem (with Ken Ludwig)
The Matchmaker
Our Town
The Skin of our Teeth

<u>Thornton Wilder One Act Series: The Ages of Man</u>
Infancy
Childhood
Youth
The Rivers Under the Earth

<u>Thornton Wilder One Act Series: The Seven Deadly Sins</u>
The Drunken Sisters
Bernice
The Wreck on the 5:25
A Ringing of Doorbells
In Shakespeare and the Bible
Someone From Assisi
Cement Hands

<u>Thornton Wilder One Act Series: Wilder's Classic One Acts</u>
The Long Christmas Dinner
Queens of France
Pullman Car Hiawatha
Love and How to Cure It
Such Things Only Happen in Books
The Happy Journey to Trenton and Camden